AF488157

Sophia's Adventure in Heaven

Written by
Sophia Love & Ruth Arias

Illustrated by
Qorina Prameswari

First hardcover edition January 2023

Book illustration and layout design by Qorina Prameswari

ISBN 979-8-9853230-3-0 (Hardcover)

Books By Love
18331 Pines Blvd
Unit #133
Pembroke Pines, FL 33029

More books available at:
www.booksbylove.com

I dedicate this book to my awesome brother Stephen and my cousins
Esther, Daniel, Jude, Matthew, Max, and Mercy.
I love you all so much!
I also dedicate this book to all the children in the world!
Always remember that you are very loved!

- Sophia Love -

Matthew 19:14 New International Version (NIV)

Jesus said, "Let the little children come to me, and do not hinder them, for the kingdom of heaven belongs to such as these."

Have you ever wondered what heaven is like? It's a magnificent place that God has prepared for all of us, His children!

Hello!
My name is Sophia Love Arias and I want to take you on an amazing adventure with Jesus to the wondrous place our Heavenly Father has created for us...Heaven!

3

On a very special night when I was only six years old, I was lying in bed saying my prayers. I quickly fell asleep and realized that Jesus was waiting for me, ready to take me on an adventure of a lifetime!

I can remember Jesus greeting me with a big smile. He extended His hand to take me along for a fun ride.

On our way up to Heaven we hopped onto moving clouds. The clouds instantly transformed into horses as we rode them happily across the sky, singing and laughing along the way.

Just up ahead there was a big shining rainbow with lots of beautiful colors. I gladly jumped on with Jesus right behind me. We slid down so fast I could hardly breathe! Oh what FUN!

7

When we got to the bottom of the rainbow we fell onto the brightest and most colorful grass filled with lovely flowers that moved and sang.

The colors were so vibrant
I couldn't believe my eyes.
The flowers danced and sang beautiful
melodies that filled the air.

9

As we walked along the pasture, we came to the most fascinating playground I had ever seen! The swings were held up by magnificent angels! Children of all ages flew up into the sky as high as they wanted to go.

The monkey bars had real monkeys hanging from them. They were very happy to see me. "Hello Sophia! Want to play?" they asked as they joyfully helped swing me across the bars!

I was elated to see bounce houses, trampolines, and slides. I could hear laughter fill the air as people enjoyed this wonderful place.

Next, we stopped at an unbelievable Bakery!
What a delight it was to see all sorts of
cookies, donuts, cupcakes, pastries, and
chocolates! Oh boy, was I happy!

Jesus was thrilled to show me around. He couldn't contain his laughter as he saw my eyes light up with unexplainable joy.

In Heaven there is so much to do! It is not at all a boring place! It is a place full of wonder and excitement no matter your age.

Jesus held my hand as we skipped and giggled all the way to the best Zoo EVER!

I could never in my wildest dreams imagine seeing what I saw at this Zoo! There were lots of different and interesting creatures everywhere we looked. There were also plants and animals I had never seen on Earth before.

I saw giraffes, elephants, bears, lions, and hippos just to name a few. All of the animals were very friendly. They spoke to each other and to us! We even got to pet them and ride them around the Zoo.

But the most exciting sight to see was
Tyrannosaurus Rex walking straight towards Jesus
and me! T-Rex stopped to greet us, and Jesus grabbed
my hand to fly us all the way up on her back.
What a thrilling ride it was! Best of all, there
wasn't even an ounce of fear in me! That's
because there is no fear in heaven, just
joy, so much JOY!

This adventure with Jesus changed my life!
I woke up the next morning feeling as if Jesus
was still right next to me. I knew then and I
know now that I am absolutely loved by God and
that I am His special daughter.

You too are very special to God! He wants us all to have a relationship with Him. He wants to be your very best friend! All you have to do is receive His love in your heart. He will guide you, love you, and be with you all the days of your life. Believe in Him and He will do incredible things!

I can't WAIT for my next adventure with Jesus!
But until then, it's your turn to go on your own
adventure with Him! I know He will surprise you!
Have fun and remember to live your life in God's
joy, in His peace, and in the fullness of His love.

Pray with me...

Dear Heavenly Father,

Thank you for sending Jesus to die on the cross for me. Thank you for loving me with an unconditional love. On this day I give you my heart and I receive Jesus as the only Lord and Savior of my life. I choose to live my life to honor and love you. I am ready to go on beautiful adventures with you. Thank you for being my best friend.

Amen.

20